Timeline of World War Two espionage

September 1939

Hitler's forces invade Poland. Britain declares war on Germany. The Second World War begins.

22nd June 1940

The new French government, led by Marshall Philippe Pétain, is forced to sign an armistice agreement with Germany.

May 1940

Germany invades and occupies France.

June 1940

From now until the end of the war, Germany and Italy control nearly all of France.

10th May 1940

Winston Churchill becomes Prime Minister of Great Britain.

June 1944

Control of France is taken back from the German army after the Allied landings.

8th May 1945

VE (Victory In Europe) Day. The Allies formally accept Germany's unconditional surrender and the war in Europe is over.

22nd July 1940

The War Cabinet in Britain agrees to set up the SOE (Special Operations Executive).

Map of occupied France in 1940

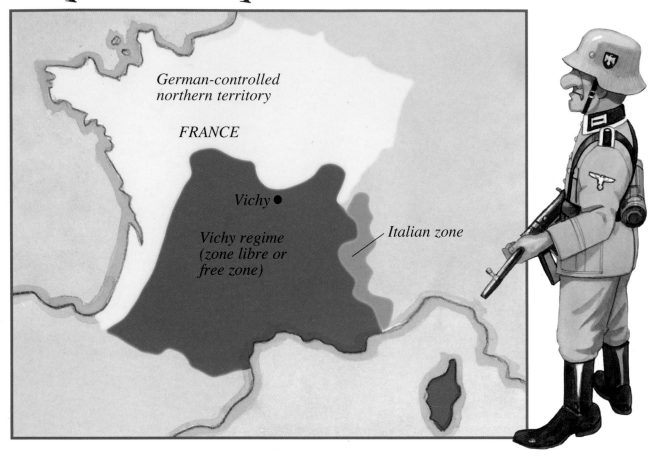

German-controlled northern territory

FRANCE

Vichy ●

Vichy regime (zone libre or free zone)

Italian zone

With its headquarters in the spa town of Vichy, the collaborationist French government was officially in control of all of France. But in reality, the 'Vichy regime' only had authority over the southern part of the country. The rest was under the control of the German army, except for small areas around the Alps border which were patrolled by their Italian allies.

The Vichy regime's territory was known as the 'zone libre', or 'free zone', until Germany decided to also seize control of this area in November 1942. At this point, France was divided into two zones fully under the control of the German military, called 'zone nord' (north zone) and 'zone sud' (south zone). It remained this way until France's liberation in 1944.

Author:
John Malam studied ancient history and
archaeology at the University of Birmingham,
England, after which he worked as an
archaeologist at the Ironbridge Gorge Museum
in Shropshire. He is now an author, specialising
in information books for children. He lives in
Cheshire with his wife and their two children.
Find out more at: www.johnmalam.co.uk

Artist:
Mark Bergin was born in Hastings, England,
in 1961. He studied at Eastbourne College of
Art and specialises in historical reconstructions,
aviation and maritime subjects. He lives in
Bexhill-on-Sea with his wife and children.

Series creator:
David Salariya was born in Dundee, Scotland.
He has illustrated a wide range of books and
has created and designed many new series for
publishers in the UK and overseas. In 1989, he
established The Salariya Book Company.

Editor:
Stephen Haynes

Editorial Assistants:
Mark Williams, Tanya Kant

Published in Great Britain in MMXVII by
Book House, an imprint of
The Salariya Book Company Ltd
25 Marlborough Place, Brighton BN1 1UB
www.salariya.com
www.book-house.co.uk
ISBN: 978-1-911242-47-5

SALARIYA

1 3 5 7 9 8 6 4 2

A CIP catalogue record for this book is available
from the British Library.

Printed and bound in China.

Visit
www.salariya.com
for our online catalogue and
fun free stuff.

PAPER FROM
SUSTAINABLE
FORESTS

You Wouldn't Want to Be a™ Secret Agent in World War Two!

Written by
John Malam

Illustrated by
Mark Bergin

Created and designed by
David Salariya

A Perilous Mission Behind Enemy Lines

BOOK HOUSE
a SALARIYA imprint

Contents

Introduction

Your country needs you! It's May 1940, and countries across Europe are fighting for survival in the Second World War. The Netherlands, Denmark and Belgium have all surrendered to Germany, and now the German army has invaded France. French cities are falling to the invaders, and German troops are moving towards Paris, the nation's capital.

As a wireless operator in the French army, your job is to send messages from your commanders to the troops. It will be a terrible day if France surrenders to Germany! What will you do then? Become a prisoner of war? Escape and become a refugee? Find a way to carry on the fight? It's your choice...

Bonjour. Je m'appelle Pascal Blanchard.
(Hello. My name is Pascal Blanchard.)

EUROPE AT WAR. The Second World War began in September 1939. The German army has swept across western Europe. Only the English Channel has stopped it – so far – from invading Britain.

May–June 1940: German advance forces British and French troops to escape across the Channel to Britain.

GREAT BRITAIN
DENMARK
THE NETHERLANDS
London
ENGLISH CHANNEL
BELGIUM
GERMANY
Paris
FRANCE
ITALY
SPAIN

Refugee! Escape to London

You will never forget Saturday, 22 June 1940. France surrendered to Germany, and you were ordered to send the bad news to French soldiers, telling them to lay down their weapons. For them, the war was over – France was beaten. But you vow to fight on. You will not surrender!

You flee to Britain, dressed as a civilian. You are one of thousands of refugees escaping from occupied Europe – but the British have to make sure you are not a German secret agent trying to sneak into the country. You are taken to London, where MI5 (the secret British Security Service) check you out. They are interested in your language skills. What could they want?

What languages do you speak?

I think this one could be quite useful to us.

Countdown to war

1921: Adolf Hitler becomes leader of the Nazi Party in Germany. By 1932 the Nazis are Germany's main political party.

1933. Hitler becomes Chancellor – leader of the German government. He plans to build a German empire to last for 1,000 years.

1936. Hitler sends troops into the Rhineland – which Germany had been forbidden to do since the end of the First World War.

1938. German troops invade Austria and a part of Czechoslovakia that had once belonged to Austria.

1 September 1939. Germany invades Poland. Britain and France declare war on Germany on 3 September.

28 June 1940. Six days after France surrenders, Hitler flies to Paris and goes on a tour of the French capital.

The words of British Prime Minister Neville Chamberlain, broadcast 3 September 1939.

11

Interviewed! But what's the job?

La France ou la Grande Bretagne?
(France or Britain?)

It feels safe in Britain at first. But when the first German bombs fall on central London during the night of 23 August 1940, you know the war is getting closer – and you want to have a part in it.

You don't have long to wait! You are asked to attend an interview at the Northumberland Hotel, London. An officer from the British army asks you lots of questions about France, about yourself, and about your work as a wireless operator. Sometimes he speaks in English, sometimes in French. It seems as though he's testing you for a job, but he doesn't give you any clue what it is.

WHICH SIDE ARE YOU ON? Only one of your parents is French – the other is British. This means you have dual nationality and can serve in either the British or the French armed forces. The choice is yours.

FREE FRENCH FORCES. If both your parents had been French, you would have had no choice but to join the Free French Forces, who are fighting to free France from the Germans.

GENERAL CHARLES DE GAULLE. A leading member of the French government, de Gaulle (right) was in London when France surrendered to Germany. He has made London his base, and has called for French soldiers to join the Free French Forces.

Cross of Lorraine

The Cross of Lorraine is the symbol of the Free French.

13

You're picked! Now set Europe ablaze!

Welcome, Second Lieutenant Blanchard. Your codename is Léon.*

Yes, sir! Thank you, sir!

* Léon means 'lion', and is a popular name in France.

You are called back for a second and then a third interview, each as puzzling as the first. It is only when you reach the end of the third interview that you find out what's going on. The British want you to become an agent in Section F (the France section) of the Special Operations Executive (SOE). It's a top-secret military group whose mission is to cause maximum disruption to the Germans. In the words of Prime Minister Winston Churchill, your job is to 'set Europe ablaze'. It sounds exciting – and dangerous!

WINSTON CHURCHILL (right) became Prime Minister of Britain on 10 May 1940. He gave Dr Hugh Dalton, the Minister of Economic Warfare, the job of setting up the Special Operations Executive. Its headquarters are in Baker Street, London.

Today, 22 July 1940, the War Cabinet has agreed to set up the SOE.

Your new job

SECRET MISSION. You'll be trained to work as an SOE agent, then sent on a dangerous mission to France. You'll either be sneaked into the country by fishing boat (let's hope you don't get seasick), or dropped by parachute.

Handy hint

Before you go on your first mission, write your will – there's a good chance you won't survive.

WIRELESS. Once you're in France, you will use your skills as a wireless operator to send and receive messages. This is risky, as the Germans might detect you.

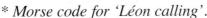

* Morse code for 'Léon calling'.

CAPTURED. If the Germans arrest you, you can expect to be interrogated to reveal your secrets. You might even be tortured.

WAAFs. It isn't only men who become SOE agents. Women are also recruited, and they join the Women's Auxiliary Air Force.

EXECUTED. If the Germans decide you are a spy (which is one way of describing you), you might be executed by firing squad.

15

The right stuff? School for danger*

You are now a student (that's what you're called) and you are about to undergo a training programme to find out if you have what it takes to be a secret agent. You will be tested by psychologists, psychiatrists and military trainers. If you fail the tests, you'll be sent home. If you pass, you'll be moved to a paramilitary school in northern Scotland, where you'll have lessons in physical exercise, fieldcraft, sabotage skills, using weapons and silent killing. There are several of these schools in the Arisaig and Morar areas of Inverness-shire – an isolated and tough terrain of mountains and lakes.

1. THE SHAKE

It's so good to see you!

Getting fit

RUNNING. You'll be sent on long runs in all weathers in full battledress. This will test your strength and general fitness.

OBSTACLE COURSE AND TUMBLING. You'll walk along a narrow wooden beam raised off the ground, and you'll practise forward rolls. This will test your balance.

ROPEWORK. You'll climb ropes and crawl across rope nets. This will test your agility.

* School for Danger *is the title of a film about the SOE made in 1947.*

2. THE TWIST

3. THE KILL

Er... what are you doing?

OK – you can stop now, sir!

Handy hint

Stay away from the bar – it's there to test you. If you get drunk, the SOE will know you can't be trusted with secrets.

COMBAT TRAINING. An instructor will teach you the technique of silent killing.
1. He will shake your hand.
2. He will twist you around.
3. He will pull a dagger and pretend to stab you.

Learning new skills

PLASTIC EXPLOSIVE. You will learn how to handle plastic explosive (PE), and how to use it to make explosive devices.

Why me?

SURVIVING IN THE WILD. You will learn how to live off the land – finding food, making fires and building shelters.

MAP, COMPASS, DAGGER. You will learn to read maps, use a compass and handle a double-edged SOE dagger.

Parachuted! Earning your wings

As part of your military training you'll be taught to parachute from an aeroplane. This is because you might be dropped into enemy territory in France at the start of a mission. You will make four or five jumps, including one at night. The training is at No.1 Parachute Training School, which is based at RAF Ringway in Cheshire, just south of Manchester. Not every student will pass the parachute training. Some will simply lose their nerve and ask to leave the course, and some will get injured and be unable to carry on. The lucky ones who pass will earn the Parachutist Badge. Take a deep breath, hold tight, jump!

BALLOON JUMP. At RAF Ringway you will make your first jump, from a box held up by a barrage balloon. It's only 215 metres (700 feet) above the ground – but it will feel much higher!

Aaaaargh!

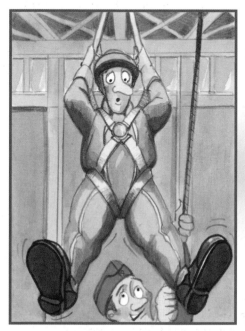

SWINGING. You will start by swinging from a roof beam, to get you ready for being off the ground.

"Get off my balloon!"

Handy hint

When you land, be sure to keep your legs together, not apart. This way you'll make a good landing and you won't break a leg.

ROLLING. You will learn how to land safely, then do a forward roll and come to a stop.

WINGS. The Parachutist Badge – your 'wings' – is what you will earn if you pass the training.

REAL JUMP 1. Your first real jump will probably be at night, from a heavy bomber such as the RAF's Handley Page Halifax. You will jump from a height of about 1,220 metres (4,000 feet).

REAL JUMP 2. Your next real jump will be in the daytime. You jump with a leg bag dangling beneath you. This is how you'll carry your equipment into France.

No more school! Training is over

Learning more new skills

LOCK-PICKING. You'll learn how to open locks without a key. This will be useful for breaking into places, and for getting out of handcuffs!

SECRET MEETINGS. You'll learn to meet your contacts without the enemy suspecting a thing.

DEAD LETTERBOX. You'll learn how to hide messages in safe places where the enemy will not find them.

The last part of your training is at Beaulieu (say 'BEW-lee'), a grand country estate in Hampshire, in the south of England. You're there for three weeks to learn how to survive as an SOE agent behind enemy lines.

The worst part of the course is the mock interrogation, when you're dragged from your bed in the middle of the night, tied to a chair and bombarded with questions by a trainer pretending to be a Nazi officer. It's meant to scare you, and it does. Whatever happens, don't give away any secrets, or you'll fail the course.

WIRELESS. You'll use your skills as a wireless operator to send and receive Morse code messages without the enemy finding out where you are.

CHECKING OUT A TARGET. You'll learn how to identify a target, such as a factory, then work out how to get inside without being caught.

SABOTAGE. You'll learn how to damage machinery and other enemy equipment so it can't be used again.

If you fail

SENT AWAY. If you fail the final stage of the training you will be a problem – you know too much. Most of all, you know the identities of the other students. It will be too risky to send you back to your real life. Instead, you will be sent to a workshop in a remote part of Scotland, far away from the nearest town. You'll stay there until all that you know is out of date and of no use to the enemy.

Goodies! Your box of tricks

S-PHONE. A wireless set for communicating by speech, not Morse code, with a plane or boat.

BICYCLE GENERATOR. Keep pedalling and it will charge the batteries of your wireless set.

As a fully trained SOE agent you have access to an amazing range of special devices for use on missions. They are top secret, and each one of them has been designed to do a specific job.

To disguise your appearance, wear false teeth and rub wrinkling cream onto your skin – this will make you look older than you really are.

Get used to working with harmless-looking objects that are really booby traps, and find out how and when to use them. If you're issued with a sleeve gun, practise firing it at a target – it might look just like a metal tube, but it packs a deadly shot and might save your life.

Learning to use a sleeve gun

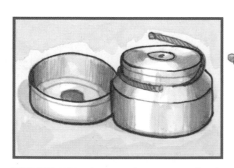

FIREPOT. A metal case packed with thermite and gunpowder. It burns with an intense heat and sets fire to whatever is nearby.

EXPLOSIVE RAT. A dead rat packed with plastic explosive. It explodes when thrown onto a fire. Best hidden amongst coal.

INCENDIARY SUITCASE. A booby-trapped suitcase that bursts into flames when opened. Leave it for the enemy to find.

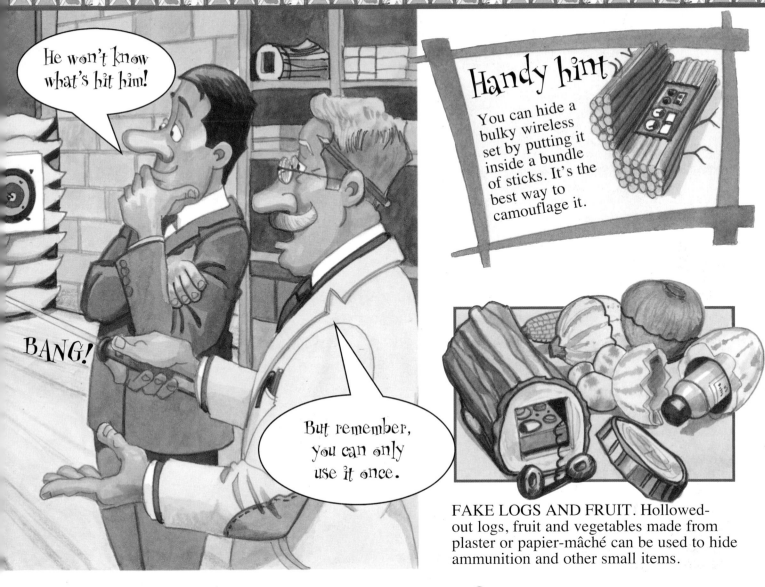

Handy hint

You can hide a bulky wireless set by putting it inside a bundle of sticks. It's the best way to camouflage it.

FAKE LOGS AND FRUIT. Hollowed-out logs, fruit and vegetables made from plaster or papier-mâché can be used to hide ammunition and other small items.

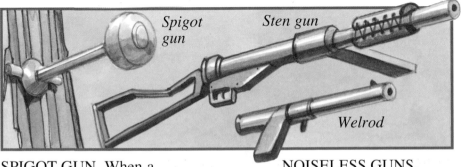

SPIGOT GUN. When a passer-by accidentally moves a wire attached to this booby trap, it fires a single bullet at them.

NOISELESS GUNS. The Sten gun has a range of about 69 metres (225 feet), the Welrod pistol about 7.3 metres (24 feet).

TRIPWIRE AND MATCHES. Steel wire is used to trip people, and slow-burning matches are for lighting fuses for explosives.

Jump! You're dropped into France

After training you go to an airbase in the east of England where you are given instructions for an 'in and out' mission to France. You are in a three-man sabotage team whose job is to raid a factory making tyres for German trucks. It's been bombed by the RAF, but it's still working, so an SOE mission is needed to wreck it for good. At night, a Whitley bomber flies low (to avoid being detected by enemy radar), and you jump when told to. At the drop zone you are met by a reception party of fighters from the French Resistance. They've been expecting you, and will help you on the mission.

The sabotage team

TEAM LEADER. He's an experienced SOE agent who has been into enemy-occupied France on missions before. Obey him.

WIRELESS OPERATOR. This is you. It's your job to keep in contact with headquarters in England. You are the team's ears.

EXPLOSIVES EXPERT. Plastic explosives, gelignite, grenades, incendiary devices, time switches and fuses are in this man's hands.

This time it's for real!

Handy hint

If you think you might be airsick, take some airsickness tablets before you leave.

Bleugh! Should've taken some airsickness tablets!

RESISTANCE FIGHTERS. These are French men and women fighting the enemy in France. They're on your side.

EQUIPMENT. Apart from the equipment you'll carry with you, everything else you'll need will be inside containers parachuted with you. Don't lose them!

Blend in! Be a good actor

The Resistance fighters collect the team's equipment, gather in the parachutes and hurry you from the drop zone. Nothing is left behind, so the Germans won't suspect anything. It's too risky to keep the team together, so the Resistance take each of you to a different hideaway. You go to a farm, where a French woman pretends to be your wife. You wear French clothes, speak French, and do nothing to draw attention to yourself. After a few days blending in, you cycle past the tyre factory. It looks like an ordinary bike ride, but what you're doing is checking out the target. There's a scary moment when German soldiers ask to see your identity papers. The papers are forged, but you hope they're good enough to fool the enemy.

FAKE FARMER. You work as if you are a farmer, but all the time you're waiting for word from the team leader about when to attack the factory.

Checking out the target

GUARDS. German soldiers guard the factory gates and patrol the perimeter fence. It's very well guarded.

ARMAMENTS. There are guns all around the factory. Some are for firing at aeroplanes, others are to be used against intruders.

WEAK POINT. You search for a weakness in the fence. When you find one, you know that it will be your way to get into the factory.

Voici mes papiers.
(Here are my papers.)

Alles ist in Ordnung.
(Everything's in order.)

Handy hint

Don't write anything down – it could be used as evidence against you. Commit everything to memory.

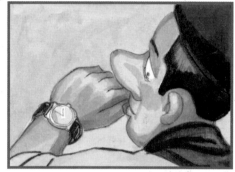

TIMETABLE. When you enter the factory, everything will have to be timed to the second. Work out exactly how long each stage will take.

TYRE STORE. Finished tyres are stored in a railway siding ready to leave the factory. You must destroy them.

Kaboom! Tonight's target

On mission day, the sabotage team comes together and the team leader goes over the timetable in detail. You check and double-check that the wireless set is working. The minutes slowly tick away, and no-one speaks. You are as nervous as the others, but try not to show it. At last it's time to go. You wait until the perimeter guards are out of sight, then dash to the fence and crawl under it. The team split up. The others head to the tyre store and set their charges. You go inside the factory to sabotage the machinery. The charges explode, and their dull thuds are followed by balls of orange fire. Sirens wail, and searchlights flash across the ground. The job's done, and it's time to leave.

Mehr Wasser!
(More water!)

Mission timetable

18:00 HOURS.** You send a coded wireless message from 'Léon' to England, asking for a pick-up plane to come at 03:45 hours.

20:00 HOURS. Check all the explosive charges. Make them ready to use by setting their fuses and time switches.

23:45 HOURS. Put camouflage paint on your face. This will make it harder for you to be spotted in the dark.

* 'Pick up at 03:45.'   ** 6:00 p.m., using the 24-hour clock. Say 'eighteen hundred hours'.

Handy hint

Put charges in the same place on each machine, so the same parts are destroyed. Then they can't use parts from one machine to repair another.

03:00 HOURS.
Mission accomplished!

01:30 HOURS. Enter the factory at the weak point you located in the perimeter fence.

01:45 HOURS. Make your way into the factory and place the explosive charges amongst the machines.

02:30 HOURS. Leave the factory. Will you make it to the pick-up place in time for the rescue plane to meet you?

Safe house! You're on the run

Within minutes of the explosions, the night sky is lit up with searchlights. The pilot of the pick-up plane decides it's too dangerous to land, and he turns around. You're stranded! All around you are the sounds of German search parties and their barking tracker dogs. The Resistance fighters take you to a safe house where you can stay until a new pick-up can be arranged.

SPLIT UP. Each agent is taken to a different safe house. This way there is less chance of everyone in the team being caught.

ON THE MOVE. You can't stay in the same safe house for too long, so the Resistance fighters move you around. You get used to being carted from place to place.

IN DANGER. The men and women of the French Resistance risk their lives to protect you. If they are caught sheltering you, they will be severely punished, and may be put to death.

31

Pick-up! It's time to leave

After a few days the tracker dogs are called off and the search parties go away. You send a wireless message to England and wait for the reply. It says a plane will be sent tonight!

After dark the Resistance fighters take you to a field where you join your comrades. The Resistance people place two rows of burning torches on the ground to mark out a temporary airstrip. Suddenly, a tiny RAF Lysander plane drops from the sky and heads for the field. It'll touch down and take off again in less than two minutes, so get ready to run up to it and climb on board. The pilot will soon have you back in England – but it won't be long before you return to France on another daring mission.

Shift yourselves!

Getting you home

KEEP IT SECRET. The fewer people know about the pick-up, the better. The pilot won't land if he thinks there's a problem.

ALL ABOARD. The Lysander carries three or four passengers at most. It's a squeeze, but you've got to get in.

GET READY. The team leader gives the OK to the pilot, who takes off as fast as he can. The Resistance fighters wave goodbye.

Handy hint

Stand by the *left* line of airstrip lights. The pilot has orders to shoot people standing in the wrong place — even you!

FLYING HIGH. The pilot flies high to avoid flak from anti-aircraft guns fired from the ground. It's a bumpy flight.

WELL DONE! You are congratulated on the success of the mission. But there's no time to relax, as you'll soon be sent on another. Good luck!

Au revoir et bonne chance. (Goodbye and good luck.)

Bon voyage! (Have a safe journey.)

33

Glossary

Airstrip A strip of ground where aircraft land and take off.

Anti-aircraft gun A large gun that fires shells from the ground at aircraft as they fly overhead.

Barrage balloon A huge balloon, tied to the ground by cables. The cables act as an obstacle to enemy aircraft.

Booby trap A hidden bomb or weapon that goes off when it is touched or moved.

Camouflage To hide objects or people by colouring them so they blend in with their background.

Chancellor The title of the German head of state.

Civilian A person who is not a member of the armed forces.

Dead letterbox A hiding place where secret messages can be left.

Drop zone The area into which parachutists are dropped.

Fieldcraft Outdoor skills such as survival techniques and map-reading.

Flak Gunfire from anti-aircraft guns.

Free French Forces An organisation of French men and women who carried on fighting after France had surrendered to Germany in 1940.

Fuse A device, usually connected to a timer, which causes a bomb to explode.

Incendiary device A device designed to cause a fire.

Interrogate To force a person to answer questions.

Leg bag A bag of equipment tied to a parachutist's leg.

MI5 Military Intelligence, Section 5 – the British Security Service.

Morse code A signalling system in which short and long sounds or flashes of light – known as 'dots and dashes' – stand for letters of the alphabet.

Nazi A member of the National Socialist German Workers' Party (the Nazi Party), which ruled Germany from 1933 to 1945.

Occupied Invaded and ruled by an enemy country.

Paramilitary Organised or carried out using military techniques.

Perimeter The outside edge of an area of land.

Psychiatrist A doctor who studies the human mind and treats a patient with medicines.

Psychologist A doctor who studies the human mind but does not treat a patient with medicines.

Radar A system for detecting moving objects in the sky, especially aircraft.

RAF The British Royal Air Force.

Reception party A group of Resistance fighters who met SOE agents when they arrived in France.

Refugee A person who leaves their own country to seek safety in another.

Resistance The small groups of French men and women who secretly fought the German forces occupying France in the Second World War.

Sabotage The deliberate act of destroying equipment and machinery.

Safe house A building where it is safe for a wanted or hunted person to hide.

Special Operations Executive (SOE) A British government organisation that began in 1940, sending specially trained agents to disrupt the country's enemies.

Thermite A powder that burns at a very high temperature.

Will A legal document giving instructions for dealing with a person's property and possessions after their death.

Wireless An old-fashioned word for 'radio'.

Index

The French Resistance

Despite the name, the French Resistance was not really a single organisation. It was a collection of small, independent groups of French people who decided to oppose the German occupation of France during the Second World War – at whatever cost.

The people who made up the Resistance came from all walks of life. Some of them, such as the Communist and Anarchist members, were politically active even before the outbreak of war. Others felt a responsibility to take a stand against the oppression and persecution of the occupying regime. These included intellectuals, aristocrats, students, and even Catholic priests.

The methods of disruption and rebellion used by the Resistance took many different forms. Violence was part of their strategy, including blowing up military facilities and killing German soldiers and French citizens who were collaborating with the enemy. But they also tried to encourage the rest of the population by publishing and handing out underground newspapers that told people to fight back and not believe the official German reports.

Famous WW2 secret agents

Ian Fleming

During the war, Ian Fleming was recruited into the Royal Navy as a personal assistant to the Director of Naval Intelligence. He quickly made a name for himself. One of his notable achievements was to help form a commando unit known as No. 30 Commando, which seized important documents from targeted enemy buildings.

After the war, Fleming experimented with writing a spy novel, *Casino Royale*, which introduced the world to the enormously popular character of James Bond. He went on to write many successful Bond novels, which in turn led to the iconic film series.

Graham Greene

The famous novelist was recruited into MI6 by his sister, who worked for the organisation. It was believed that his fame, wealth and taste for globe-trotting would enable him to gather vital information. During the Second World War, he was sent to Sierra Leone in Africa. His experiences fed into his novels, which are often about the murky world of government agents and the power struggles that take place between different countries.

Kazimierz Leski

Originally trained as an engineer, Leski became an intelligence officer in the Home Army, Poland's primary resistance movement during the Second World War. By disguising himself as a German officer, he was able to cross borders without detection, spy on German construction projects and smuggle people out of German prisons. Leski is credited with undertaking at least 25 journeys across occupied Europe whilst in disguise.

Morse code

Morse code was a popular method of sending secret messages during the Second World War because it was easy to learn and could be sent using sound or light signals.

The code translates each letter of the alphabet into a unique series of dots (short sounds or flashes) and dashes (longer sounds or flashes), which can be put together to form words and sentences.

If you and your friends know the code for each letter, you could try sending secret messages to each other using Morse code.

A: • —
B: — • • •
C: — • — •
D: — • •
E: •
F: • • — •
G: — — •
H: • • • •
I: • •
J: • — — —
K: — • —
L: • — • •
M: — —
N: — •
O: — — —
P: • — — •
Q: — — • —
R: • — •

S: • • •
T: —
U: • • —
V: • • • —
W: • — —
X: — • • —
Y: — • — —
Z: — — • •
1: • — — — —
2: • • — — —
3: • • • — —
4: • • • • —
5: • • • • •
6: — • • • •
7: — — • • •
8: — — — • •
9: — — — — •
10: — — — — —